The Truth, The Lies, and the Fundraisers

An Essay on Convicted Child Killer Darlie Routier

Brenda Irish Heintzelman

The Truth, The Lies, and the Fundraisers

An Essay on Convicted Child Killer Darlie Routier

On June 6, 1996 at 2:31 a.m. Darlie Routier dialed 911 to report that an intruder had just broken into her Rowlett, Texas home and fatally stabbed two of her children. The intruder also slashed her throat, stabbed her on the arm, and even removed her panties. And according to Darlie she slept through it all.

Of course, there was never any intruder. Seven months later Darlie Routier was convicted of capital murder and sent to death row.

Twenty years later Darlie continues to sit on death row while her appeals slowly meander their way through court. In the meantime, her few but faithful followers insist that if they could just collect a little more money then surely they would be able to prove that Darlie did not murder her children. One recent fundraiser promised that as soon as the latest round of lab results were known that surely Darlie would be set free. Instead when the test results were finally released her faithful followers soon asked the court to seal them. And the only thing that was released were the details of her next fundraiser.

If only. If only they can raise more money and get more tests done. If only. If only they can raise more money then surely they will be able to prove Darlie is innocent.

There's just one problem. Darlie isn't innocent. She is guilty as sin.

The first fundraiser was launched within mere hours of Darlie's 911 call to report that her children had been murdered. At the time, the couple claimed they did not have any financial worries. If you listened to Darlie's husband back then you would believe he was really raking in the dough. But he wasn't. In fact his business was going downhill fast. He started his company just a few years earlier by taking a few of his previous employer's customers with him when he left. And around the time of the murders his biggest customer was about to leave him. The Friday before the murders Darlie's husband was begging one of his customers to give him some money even though the customer had yet to be properly billed. And just one week before the murders Darlie's husband was turned down by the bank for a $5,000 loan.

But no matter how broke they were they continued to live high on the hog. And they both pretended to others and quite possibly even to themselves that they were successful. But they weren't. They also held life insurance policies on their children which would have covered any funeral or burial expenses. So the idea there should be a fundraiser started within hours of the murders seemed strange to many people considering the couple did not appear to have any financial difficulties. The fundraiser asked for help in covering "expenses".

The following week Darlie threw a party out at the cemetery. According to a court watcher who has researched the Routier case ad nauseam, Darlie swung a sweet deal with the reporters which required they pay big money, as in many thousands of dollars, in order to attend the party and to be able to interview her. During her interview she smiled and laughed and snapped her gum for the cameras for forty-five minutes straight. She couldn't stop talking. She couldn't stop smiling. And at the end of the day as the cameras rolled Darlie couldn't stop laughing while she enjoyed spraying silly string on her sons' shared grave. At one point she said to the reporter that if he knew her sons then he would know they were up in heaven having a big party too.

She didn't cry. She didn't faint. She didn't sob for her children who had just been murdered. Instead the footage showed a woman who seemed downright happy. Her mother would later say that she was heavily drugged that day so of course she wouldn't have cried. But the same court watcher who says that Darlie raked in big money from the reporters for her interview also claims that in his research he learned Darlie's dose of Xanax was the lowest possible. Surely a starter dose of Xanax cannot mask the grief any mother would have felt so soon after two of her children were so brutally murdered. Unless, of course, she was the person who murdered them and she was thinking she was in the clear.

The video clip which showed Darlie laughing and spraying silly string at her party would later serve to do her in because when the prosecutor saw the video clip on the evening news he knew in his gut that something just wasn't right. To him it seemed her stories were changing and her behavior clearly was not consistent with what one would expect from a grieving mother. The prosecutor called the investigators and asked again what the mother's story was. The investigators brought Darlie in again for yet another police interview.

The next day during what would be Darlie's last police interview the investigator accused her of murdering her children. In response Darlie would just shrug her shoulders as if to say she either didn't know or didn't care. Then finally the seasoned investigator got the closest thing to a confession that Darlie was willing to give. She told the investigator that if she did kill her children she didn't remember it. Darlie was placed under arrest and charged with murder.

Lo and behold as soon as Darlie was placed under arrest it appeared her wonder drug suddenly wore off. For the first time since her children were murdered Darlie appeared in front of the cameras as a grief stricken sobbing devastated young woman. She couldn't stop crying. Her smile had suddenly disappeared from her face which finally began to show signs of actual grief. Her grief of course had nothing to do with her children being murdered and everything to do with getting caught.

Seven months later the "silly string video" would surface again at her trial. After the jury found Darlie guilty of capital murder one juror appeared on the Leeza Gibbons show and admitted that during deliberations they watched the "silly string video" over and over again.

Did the video convict Darlie? Of course not. There was plenty of physical evidence to show that Darlie had been lying to the investigators all along. But it helped the jurors to see the face of the defendant shortly after her children were murdered and what they saw was the face of a murderer.

After the murders but before her arrest Darlie was downright talkative. She seemed downright happy. One day she and her husband returned to the house to take the stuffed animals and cards that were left by sympathetic strangers. One neighbor watched in horror while Darlie tossed the stuffed animals one by one to her husband then cheered each time as if she was a high school sophomore at a basketball game and her team had just scored a three point shot.

Another day before her arrest but right after one of her police interviews at the Rowlett Police Station Darlie raced out into the waiting room and literally hopped right onto her mother's lap.

Another day after the murders when Darlie and one of her friends returned to the house her friend asked if there was something Darlie should tell her. Darlie ignored the question and began to complain about how much money it was going to take to whip the house back into shape.

Another day after the murders Darlie went door to door in her neighborhood to invite people to the party she was planning to hold at the cemetery.

Clearly, Darlie was not exhibiting the behavior of a mother who had just lost her children. But if you consider her behavior from the perspective of her guilt then it appears she was actually behaving in a manner consistent with a woman who thought she was literally getting away with murder. Any one of the incidents taken alone perhaps is irrelevant. But taken together the pattern certainly suggests that Darlie Routier was guilty of killing her children and that she was narcissistic enough to believe that she would get away with it.

One of her closest friends contacted me after I wrote "Unbelievable" which was my first essay on the Darlie Routier case. The caller told me that Darlie admitted she murdered her children not only to the person who called me but also to her husband and to her mother. If this is true then of course the question begs why on earth the person who called me didn't tell the police investigators as soon as Darlie had admitted what she had done. I was told that the person was threatened by Darlie's husband to keep silent and that the person was in fear of losing their life.

So if this person is telling the truth then it means the family held their fundraisers knowing full well that Darlie was guilty. The day of the murders her family tried to get money to help with "expenses". Then according to the person who has spent many years researching the case the family raked in thousands of dollars from the reporters who covered the party at the cemetery. And then just a couple of weeks later after Darlie was arrested her family held another fundraiser right at the jail where she was locked up.

But when the locals heard about the fundraiser rally being planned to be held over at the jail, they became angry according to one Rowlett, Texas resident. According to the person who contacted me about the fundraiser at the jail everyone in town believed Darlie was guilty. I was told that Darlie was known to yell at her children to get the hell out of the house. I was told that Darlie was known to make all three children, including the baby, stay out in the parking lot while she would go inside her husband's shop. I was told that the day before the murders that the older boy begged to not have to go home and the younger boy begged to be able to leave.

So the Rowlett, Texas residents who became angry decided to hold a little rally of their own. According to the person who contacted me the parallel fundraiser was a huge success while the fundraiser for Darlie at the jail was practically a no show. So Darlie's fundraiser at the jail didn't go so well but that didn't seem to stop them. Next they planned a big yard sale fundraiser to help with Darlie's legal fees.

But wait just a minute.

Darlie's lawyer was court appointed and paid for by the state.

Darlie's husband would later claim that he had to sell everything he owned in order to pay for Darlie's legal fees. But par for the course in the Darlie case that wasn't exactly the truth. In fact, a few months after the murders when Darlie's husband paid a private lawyer a $100,000 retainer fee by that time not only had the family already been collecting money from their fundraisers but they had also secured the financial backing of a local businessman who was very wealthy.

There was just one little problem with their wealthy donor. Before long he told them that Darlie and her husband both had to take polygraph tests in order for him to continue giving them money to help cover the cost of her defense.

Darlie's husband failed his polygraph exam. And so did Darlie.

She stammered with the word "inconclusive" regarding her own polygraph exam as if she had never heard the word before. That was part of Darlie's charm at the time. She would tilt her head, she would bat those heavily mascaraed lashes. She would bring out the best fake southern belle drawl she could muster. Then she would try to act all naïve and confused.

In con clu sive? Well, that's what she was told.

So when the wealthy businessman stopped funding the Routiers the family was back to square one. Please help. Darlie is innocent. She was unfairly targeted by the police investigators. The investigators didn't know what they were doing. The prosecutor was out to get her. Poor Darlie.

And well meaning kind hearted strangers responded by sending in whatever money they could afford to send.

The Routier home was soon lost to foreclosure since by the time of the murders Darlie and her husband were already behind on their mortgage payments. The amount they still owed on the mortgage was more than the house was even worth. What this means in real estate lingo is they had zero equity in their house. Darlie's husband's car was old and in need of repairs. Their boat was the same story as their house and the old car. They owed more on the boat than it was worth and it needed repairs too.

So when Darlie's husband says he had to sell everything in order to cover the costs of Darlie's defense of course his comments beg the question of just what it was that he was able to sell.

They were behind on their taxes. They were behind on their rent for her husband's shop. They were behind on their American Express payments. They were behind behind behind yet they were planning to take two big vacations in the coming month with less than twelve hundred dollars to their name. No wonder Darlie's husband asked the bank for $5,000. And no wonder the bank turned him down.

So for her husband to try to claim they were flush with funding it appears Darlie isn't the only liar in the Routier family. Nowhere in their financial scheme does it appear they would have been able to come up with the $100,000 they gave to the lawyer. And nowhere in their financial scheme did it appear they had anything close to that amount in assets. Ever. In fact, upon closer inspection it seems the couple was already in financial ruins.

Which brings us right back to the fundraisers.

And back to that yard sale.

One of the big stories her faithful few followers like to tell is that the police not only unfairly targeted Darlie in the investigation but they also failed to properly process the crime scene evidence. According to Darlie's followers the police investigators failed to secure vital evidence from the sofa Darlie claimed she was sleeping on when the phantom intruder supposedly slashed her throat.

What her followers fail to mention is that the sofa they are pointing to was scrubbed clean and sold at one of their yard sale fundraisers. The sofa wasn't scrubbed clean by the police investigators. It was scrubbed clean by Darlie's family and sold at the yard sale fundraiser.

Let that one sink in for a minute.

Two little boys had just lost their lives. Supposedly there was a psycho running around town randomly breaking into homes and killing innocent children. Clearly if

Darlie's mother and her husband both believed this was true then there is no way in hell they would have ever sold that sofa at a yard sale. No way. At all. Ever.

They would have insisted that the sofa be thoroughly examined for any trace of evidence which would help them find the monster who murdered two innocent children. But instead they scrubbed it clean and sold it.

Twenty years later if you dare speak up and point out that little detail to her facebook followers that it was the family, not the police, who disposed of the so called evidence on the sofa they will attack you.

Because it appears they do not want the truth to be known. After all their fundraisers may come to a screeching halt if word gets out that it was Darlie's own family that destroyed the evidence they claim could have cleared her.

If only... if only they can collect just a little more money then surely they can prove that poor little Darlie was unfairly targeted by the big mean police officers and the overly zealous prosecutors too.

When I wrote "Unbelievable" before it was even available for sale negative book reviews were posted on Amazon by her handful of supporters. The first person who posted a negative book review claimed she was Darlie's mother. She lied and said she had already read the essay. She hadn't. She lied and said that the essay was full of lies. It wasn't. And she threatened to sue me which of course she never did because she knew damn well the essay was true.

The harassment continues anytime anyone dares to speak up and point out the truth. In my opinion the reason her few supporters are so aggressive toward anybody who is willing to disclose the facts of the case is because they do not want their income stream to stop. Because even though they lost their biggest donor after failing the lie detector tests, or as Darlie puts it her test was "inconclusive", there have been plenty of other generous donors along the way. And it appears that her faithful few followers choose to bully anyone who gets in their way in order to try to keep their fundraisers going.

In one of her fundraisers donors are assured that even if they don't have very much money that's okay. Every little bit helps. Even if all they can send is $5.00 for Darlie's commissary fund then they just might be lucky enough to get an actual thank you note signed by Darlie herself.

Aren't there laws against convicted murderers being able to rake in money based on the notoriety of their cases? But of course in response Darlie's followers claim that she doesn't see a penny of the money that her donors send in. They insist that every penny goes directly to her lawyers. And if you question her lawyer? If you send her lawyer an email and ask how much money has been collected over the years and what it is used for then her lawyer is quick to respond and then to send copies of the emails right on to Darlie's mother. Darlie's mother will then quickly post parts of email correspondence right on facebook. Not the entire email. Just the parts that make it look like her fundraising efforts are on the up and up.

How's that saying go? Something about a skunk in the woodpile? Why on earth would Darlie's lawyer respond to a stranger in the first place? And why on earth would her lawyer immediately forward the correspondence directly to Darlie's mother?

Maybe because during one post conviction interview Darlie's mother told the reporter that she "works" for Darlie.

Is it possible that Darlie's mother is an actual employee who is being paid an actual paycheck? Is it possible that her paycheck comes directly from the money they rake in from the fundraisers?

If so then it seems that the authorities in Texas should investigate how much money has been collected on behalf of a convicted child killer and that a full disclosure should be made public as to where all of that money went.

Because if one penny of the donations has been lining Darlie's pockets or the pockets of any of her family members then it seems reasonable that the judge in Darlie's case should order that Darlie is no longer allowed to use her notoriety from being a convicted child killer in order to secure an income flow from sympathetic strangers.

~

Darlie Routier said that when she opened her eyes she saw a man standing near her feet. She didn't scream. Her husband was sleeping right upstairs in the master bedroom where the couple's youngest son was safely tucked in his crib. Her husband was tall and muscular. Her husband owned guns. Yet, according to Darlie, when she opened her eyes and saw a man standing at her feet she didn't make a sound. Instead she quietly stood up then followed behind the intruder as he slowly walked through the house toward the garage.

He didn't run. He didn't race out the front door. He didn't attack Darlie once he realized she would certainly be able to identify him to the police. According to Darlie, not only did the intruder see that she was still alive and would therefore be able to identify him he also chose to leave the murder weapon behind. That's her story and she is sticking to it. According to Darlie as she was quietly walking behind the intruder he dropped the murder weapon on the floor of the laundry room then proceeded to continue walking through the house toward the garage. Without making a sound, without screaming, without grabbing the phone and dialing 911, Darlie claimed that she quietly picked up the knife, she walked back to the kitchen, and she set the bloody knife on the kitchen counter.

According to Darlie, when the intruder entered her home she had been sleeping on the sofa in the main floor family room. She said that her children had fallen asleep on the floor in front of the still playing big screen T.V. just a few feet away from her. After setting the knife on the kitchen counter Darlie must have glanced over at her children and realized they were both badly injured. After setting the knife on the counter Darlie said she realized she had blood on her nightshirt. It was then at that moment after seeing that blood was everywhere that finally Darlie decided to let out a scream.

Bull.

At one point Darlie would tell the police investigators that one of her children had woken her up by saying "Mommy" as he stood next to her and touched her arm. She said that after she opened her eyes and saw the intruder standing near her feet that her son walked behind her as she followed the intruder through the house. Darlie said that after placing the bloody butcher knife on the kitchen counter and realizing that her children had been stabbed that she told her son to lay down on his stomach, to lay still, and to "hold on". However due to the serious nature of his injuries it is highly doubtful he would have been able to walk or to speak.

Remember that up to this point Darlie hadn't made a sound. She didn't scream when her children were brutally attacked within just a few feet of her. She didn't scream when her own throat was slashed or when her arm was stabbed or when the intruder removed her panties. She didn't scream when she saw a man standing at her feet. She didn't scream when she saw that the man was holding a bloody butcher knife. She didn't scream while the man walked through her house toward the garage. She didn't scream when she picked up the bloody butcher knife that the intruder chose to leave behind. She didn't scream when she realized that her sons were fatally injured. She didn't scream when she saw that her nightshirt was covered in blood.

Nope. According to Darlie it wasn't until after she set the bloody butcher knife on the kitchen counter that she finally decided to let out a scream.

Another one of Darlie's stories was that she was fighting off the intruder. Yet, that's not the story she gave in her written statement to the police investigators just a couple of days after the murders. She changed her story to say that what she said on the 911 call wasn't that she was fighting. What she insisted she said on the 911 call was that she was "frightening". I'll bet she was.

According to her husband he was sound asleep in the second floor master bedroom when suddenly he heard Darlie scream out his name. He said that she screamed his name three times in a row. But other times her husband said that Darlie screamed out the name of their oldest son three times in a row.

Either way, regardless of whose name she supposedly screamed, according to both Darlie and her husband at some point Darlie screamed.

When Darlie's husband heard her scream, he raced down the stairs from the master bedroom immediately. It's interesting to note however that he didn't run to Darlie. He didn't ask her why she screamed. He didn't grab the phone and dial 911 as soon as he realized there was blood everywhere. He didn't wrap his arms around her or even speak to her at all. He would later say he didn't even realize that she was also injured. He said he raced directly to his older son's badly bleeding body and began to perform CPR. Then, according to Darlie's husband, his first attempt at rescue breathing resulted in blood spurting all over him from his son's chest cavity.

It seems very strange that if his wife screamed suddenly in the middle of the night and he came racing down the stairs that he wouldn't have run right to his wife first. For this reason, I suspect that he isn't being truthful. This is what I think may have happened. I think that possibly when Darlie was stabbing their children that her children screamed and that her children's screams woke up her husband. I think he heard his children screaming and that he raced down those stairs as fast as he could to try to save them from their own mother's rage. I think he got to her after she had already fatally stabbed their oldest son but while she was still attacking their younger son. I think he grabbed her and I think when he grabbed her that she threatened him with the knife.

I think he was somehow able to calm her down and then she went into the kitchen by the sink and proceeded to slash her own throat.

Darlie had bruises on her arms which nobody can seem to explain since the issue of whether Darlie actually ever fought off her phantom attacker is always in dispute. But if my hunch is right and her husband grabbed her and wrestled her away from their children when she was attacking them then it would serve to explain how she got those bruises on her arms.

I personally don't believe that her husband had any idea what she was going to do though it could certainly be argued that he should have known it wasn't safe for their children to be left alone with her. Just one month prior to the murders, Darlie wrote a note to her children that started with "Forgive me for what I am about to do". Her husband would later say the she just had the "baby blues". Darlie would later say that she was contemplating suicide. But what if the truth is that Darlie had already been planning to murder their children?

One of her closest friends urged Darlie's husband to get her the help she so desperately needed. According to the friend ever since the birth of her third baby Darlie wasn't acting normal. And according to Darlie herself she was downright miserable. On the stand at her trial the prosecutor asked Darlie why she was so miserable and she quietly answered "I don't know".

Right after the murders the couple denied they were having any problems but again I think it's pretty safe to assume they were both lying. They were broke. His business was not flourishing as it had at first. They were spenders. They were vacationers. They were both very much into the jewelry and the parties and keeping up the appearances of being successful. But they weren't successful. They were living on borrowed money and their borrowing power had suddenly disappeared.

There's one more interesting little twist to their home life. It seemed that Darlie always had other people at the house with her when her husband was at work. Was that a coincidence or did her husband plan it that way? For example, she was a stay at home mom with three children. Yet she needed housekeepers to spend the entire day with her? And even with the housekeepers and the teenage babysitters who would hang out at the Routier home and Darlie's own sister who had been staying at the house for at least a couple of weeks leading up to the murders the photos of the crime scene do not show a house that is neat and tidy. At all.

So could it be that her husband knew Darlie was in trouble? Could it be that he was already concerned for the safety of his children? Could it be that he kept people at the house with her to make sure his children were safe?

Also, why did her sister suddenly have to leave just hours before the children were murdered? It was after nine o'clock at night. She had been staying right at the house and working with Darlie's husband during the day. Then suddenly Darlie's husband took her sister to an apartment where her sister sometimes stayed with her boyfriend. That's a completely different twist to the story. Her sister was just fifteen years old but not living with her mother and her step-father? Why? Instead she would go back and forth between her boyfriend's apartment and Darlie's house.

And then just a few hours before the murders suddenly after staying two whole weeks straight with Darlie her sister demanded to be taken to her boyfriend's apartment after nine o'clock at night? Why? Could it be that Darlie and her husband were already arguing and her sister wanted to get the heck out of there? Could it be that Darlie and her husband were arguing about her sister?

From this perspective I think it's reasonable to consider the possibility that Darlie's husband knew more than he was telling the police investigators. I think from this perspective that it's reasonable to consider the possibility that Darlie's husband caught her in the act of murdering their children then tried to stage the crime scene to make it appear as if his family had been attacked by a stranger.

Again, I think it's possible that he heard his children scream, he raced down the stairs, he stopped her but not before it was too late, then she turned the knife on him. I think there was a struggle and he somehow got her to calm down then she suddenly raced to the kitchen and slashed her throat while standing at the kitchen sink.

I think her husband got to work fast trying to stage the crime scene in order to try to protect Darlie from being blamed for killing their children. I know that sounds really strange but if he was a man full of guilt for not having protected his children then maybe he figured he would at least try to protect his wife. Maybe he blamed himself for what happened to his children. Maybe he planned to try to get Darlie the help she needed. But first he would need to try to convince the police investigators that she didn't do it.

He said that when he heard Darlie scream that he raced down the stairs and ran directly over to where his oldest was bleeding to death on the floor of the family room. He said he began to perform CPR but that rescue breathing caused blood to spurt all over him from his son's chest cavity. Darlie and her husband both said that while he was performing CPR that she grabbed the phone and dialed 911. Her husband would later say that he found out what had happened simply by listening to his wife as she spoke with the 911 operator.

Does any of this sound normal? Does it sound like the truth?

Of course not.

Instead I think this scenario is plausible – I think the couple argued. I think the sister demanded to leave. I think when he returned to the house the couple argued some more. He finally grew tired of the arguing and told her he wanted a divorce as he walked up the stairs at around one a.m. leaving his two older children sleeping on the floor within just a few feet of Darlie who was on the sofa in the family room. I think she refused to go upstairs to bed and wanted to keep right on arguing. And he said no and proceeded to keep walking up those stairs.

I think when he walked away from her she became filled with rage.

I don't think Darlie was okay with the thought of a divorce or of having to be a single mother. I don't think Darlie ever intended on having to work. And I don't think Darlie believed she would necessarily get custody either. I think at some point she said to her friend that she didn't want to get help because if she left her children with her mother-in-law while she got help then it wouldn't look good for her down the road in a custody battle. So I think when he walked away from her he probably threatened to take custody of the children and told her she would be out the door.

I think she became furious with her husband for walking away from her and for threatening divorce and saying that he would take custody of their children.

According to Darlie her husband walked up those stairs at one a.m. At 2:31 Darlie dialed 911. So in considering she had ninety-one minutes alone with her children I think this is what happened. I think when her husband was walking up the stairs that both he and Darlie were still saying mean words to each other. I think she probably told him to go to hell. I think she probably tried to act tough and maybe she even laughed at him when he said he would take custody of their children.

I think Darlie was physically, emotionally, and mentally exhausted. I think that her hormones were probably out of whack and that the diet pills she was popping probably weren't helping her either.

Summer vacation had just started and I think the thought of having her rambunctious seven year old home all day instead of being at school was more than she could bear.

She was supposed to leave on a big family vacation the following week but she had no money. In a few weeks she was supposed to be taking a solo vacation to Mexico without her husband and children. Not only was she broke she also believed she was fat. Remember, she was taking diet pills. So her big plan to vacation in Cancun must have seemed an impossible dream.

I think Darlie was feeling trapped. Her husband had been driving her car back and forth to work since his car was in need of repairs. So she was left at home all day with three kids and no car. And I think it made her angry.

She was known as "shop til she drops Darlie" but her credit card payment was overdue.

I think the heat was getting to her too. I think her period was due since the murders occurred exactly four weeks after the day her husband came home early from work and found her in bed with her supposed suicide note addressed to her children. She would later say that just a couple of days later her period started and she felt normal again.

I think when Darlie's husband went up those stairs she was broke, she was hormonal, she was frightened, she was angry, and she was downright miserable. And

I think when her husband threatened to take custody of the children and told her she'd have to move out I think her fears and her sadness turned to rage.

I think she was angry. I think she was in rage over the fact that when he walked up those stairs she realized she could no longer control him with her threats and her tears.

After he went upstairs I think she tried to go to sleep but instead she just laid there on the sofa in the family room and cried. And when she was tired of crying I think she thought about all of the nasty words her husband had just said to her and she decided she would take revenge.

I believe she decided to kill their children.

I think she cried some more when she realized what she was thinking. I think she sobbed for perhaps a half hour or so. I think she struggled with herself about whether or not to murder her children. I think she tried to keep control of her senses but her rage was stronger than she was. I think she hated herself when she realized what she was thinking. But I think she hated losing control of her husband even more.

I think she sobbed some more and then slowly drifted off to sleep.

I think that shortly after Darlie fell asleep that her younger son woke up and tugged on her arm to wake her up.

And at that moment I think all of the rage inside of her came flooding to the surface again.

I think she walked out to the kitchen and took the murder weapon from her knife collection. According to her housekeeper Darlie had been sharpening her knives the afternoon before she murdered her children.

I think Darlie took one of her sharpened knives and returned to the family room where she proceeded to stab her oldest son. I think he screamed. And I think her younger son screamed too. And at that moment I think her husband came running down the stairs.

I think he struggled with Darlie to get her to stop stabbing their children. I think she ran to the kitchen and slashed her own throat. I think when they both thought that both of their sons were already dead that her husband took the murder weapon and one of his socks which had the boys' blood and Darlie's DNA on it outside to dispose of them down the sewer drain. In his shock and disbelief I think he was able to put the knife down the sewer drain but didn't realize he had dropped the sock in the yard.

I think when he returned inside the house he had to once again stop Darlie from stabbing their children. I think during this struggle Darlie's arm was cut. I think when she finally set the knife down on the counter he had convinced her their children were dead.

I think that he was covered in blood from wrestling the knife away from Darlie. So he had to come up with a reason why he had blood on him. I think that's why he talked so much about giving one of his son's CPR. Surely if blood spurted from the little boy's chest cavity then he would not have continued to try to give him CPR.

I think that he told Darlie to dial 911 in order to keep her away from their children. And I think in Darlie's mind she realized that she was once again in control.

Darlie dialed 911 and proceeded to spend over six minutes hanging on the phone while her children lay dying right before her eyes and while her husband gave the appearance to the first responding officers that he was trying to help his children.

When the first officer arrived he told Darlie to get off the phone and to help her children. She ignored him.

I think she stayed right on the phone so she could get her story told on a recorded line.

Three minutes and thirty seconds after Darlie dialed 911 the family dog finally started barking. He started barking because that's when the police officers were first entering the home.

Had there been an intruder surely the dog would have barked as soon as the intruder had entered the Routier home. Also as soon as the officers arrived and walked by the garage where the phantom intruder had supposedly entered and exited the home the security lights went on. Because the sensors for the security lights were directly above where the Routiers claimed the intruder had walked.

There's more. The screen in the garage was sliced in a very neatly cut T pattern. And one of the knives from the Routier home was found to have shards of screen material on it.

There's more. When the police officers were at the house and the EMTs were tending to the children Darlie's husband told the officers to check out how beautiful his wife was. No kidding. He even pointed out her breast implants. He went on to say how much he loved his wife.

None of this is normal.

Then while standing with Darlie before she was placed into the ambulance her husband told her that her panties were missing. Darlie said she didn't realize it until he mentioned it to her.

Also it should be noted that when the EMTs first checked Darlie out her blood pressure and pulse rate were not elevated.

~

Twenty years later Darlie's faithful followers are now claiming that they believe Darlie's husband is the person who murdered her children.

That's right. Twenty years later they are suddenly trying to make a case against him. Even though Darlie insisted at the time that she saw the intruder and that the intruder was not her husband. Even though Darlie insisted at the time that when she screamed her husband immediately came running down the stairs from the master bedroom. Even though Darlie was convicted of capital murder and sent to death row without saying a word that would make anyone believe that her husband had anything to do with the murders. Her followers are still insisting that Darlie's husband is the person who belongs on death row.

They claim that Darlie's lawyer was forced by her husband to not implicate him at trial. Baloney.

They claim that Darlie was somehow drugged by her husband while he stabbed their children and slashed her throat. Baloney.

They claim that he thought he had killed her and was surprised to see that she had survived. Baloney.

If Darlie's husband is guilty of anything it is that he possibly tried to cover up his wife's crimes. Perhaps he felt guilty for leaving the boys alone with her down on the main floor instead of making sure they were safely tucked in their beds. Perhaps he felt guilty for ignoring her cries for help one month earlier when she wrote a note to her children "Forgive me for what I'm about to do" then claimed she was contemplating suicide.

Perhaps he figured he would do his best to keep her from going to prison and to get her the help she so obviously needed.

Perhaps he did lie to the police to cover up for Darlie's crimes. But to think that he committed the crimes then somehow framed Darlie seems downright ludicrous. As Darlie's husband so clearly stated in a post conviction interview there's just no way she would be sitting in prison if she thought for a second that it was him who killed their children.

Her followers' claims that the killer was actually Darlie's husband reeks eerily similar to one of Darlie's many appeal efforts within a few years of her conviction. According to Darlie her husband was attempting to hire someone to break into their home, to steal a few items, and then to get paid off when they collected from the insurance company. Her husband even signed an affidavit to that effect.

And her mother said she remembered the day when they came to her house then left abruptly when Darlie became angry with her husband for talking about wanting to find someone to break into their home so they could pull off an insurance scam.

If any of this is true then shame on all four of them. Darlie, her husband, and her mother and step-father too. If it's true then it means that after two precious little boys lost their lives that the four people who should have loved them the most of anyone on the planet all kept their mouths shut instead of telling the police investigators everything they knew. The boys' own mother, the boys' own father, the boys' own grandmother and their step-grandfather all would have known that a plot was forming for a stranger to break into their home. Yet not one of them bothered to tell the police investigators about it.

Then years later when it was time to file an appeal all four of them were very open about the supposed plot to find someone to break in. Use your common sense. It is simply not reasonable to believe that all four of them would have refused to tell the police investigators about it at the time of the murders.

So the story goes. Her faithful few followers' sudden claim that her husband committed the murders is gaining momentum perhaps parallel to another fundraising effort. Because remember folks, if only, if only they can collect more money then surely she will be set free.

If you want to believe Darlie's intruder story then you would have to believe that somehow the intruder was able to enter and exit the home directly under the security light sensors without activating the lights. But the lights were in working order so clearly Darlie was lying.

If you want to believe Darlie then you would have to believe the family dog never barked at the intruder. But as soon as the officers arrived at the crime scene the dog started to bark so clearly Darlie is lying.

If you want to believe Darlie's story then you would have to believe that she actually slept through the attack.

If you want to believe Darlie's story then you would have to believe that she slept through two of her children being brutally attacked within just a few feet of her.

If you want to believe Darlie's story then you would have to believe that the intruder knew he was leaving an eye witness behind along with the murder weapon which by the way did not have any fingerprints on it.

There's more. Once Darlie realized the police officers had removed her kitchen sink for testing her story included her wetting towels to place on her children's stab wounds. In fact, the police investigators believe that Darlie stood at the kitchen sink when she slashed her own throat.

If you want to believe Darlie's story then you would have to believe that when she opened her eyes and saw a stranger standing near her feet that she didn't scream. That she quietly walked behind him. That she picked up the bloody butcher knife when he dropped it on the floor.

If you want to believe Darlie's story then you would have to believe that some psychotic monster chose the house on the block with the television still on to sneak in and murder two innocent children.

If you want to believe Darlie's story then you would have to believe that the person who contacted me was lying when they told me that as soon as they heard the news they knew in their heart that it was Darlie herself who killed her children.

If you want to believe Darlie's story then you would have to believe that the person who contacted me to tell me that Darlie admitted killing her children was lying too.

If you want to believe her faithful few followers' story that her husband killed their children then you would have to believe that for twenty years Darlie has chosen to sit silently on death row while her husband has remarried and moved on with his life.

In my opinion, Darlie Routier killed her children. I think the jury got it right. And I think if she were a man that she would have been executed by now. I think if she were a man that the court would have prevented her from holding any fundraisers. And I think if she were a man that kind hearted strangers would not be paying their hard earned money into her commissary account.

I do not support the death penalty. But the voters in Texas do. And because of the crimes Darlie committed, her jury sentenced her to death.

As the prosecutor in Darlie's case has stated, "There's no intruder there's no mystery killer".

"She is always going to portray herself as a victim of some injustice."

"...they've (the Routier family) been free to make whatever claim they want to. To distort the evidence as they see fit. To rewrite the testimony at trial. I've heard claims about fingerprints and they fail to back those claims up. I've heard claims about DNA, they don't back those claims up. About every five years there's another new unexplained claim that comes up from the family but they never ever produce any evidence that undermines that jury's verdict in this case".

First they tried to say the police investigators unfairly targeted Darlie. But those investigators followed up on every lead.

Then they said the investigators didn't take evidence from the sofa. But they're the ones who sold it.

Then they claimed that Darlie didn't know she was a suspect when she spoke with the police. The truth is Darlie acknowledged the Miranda warning in writing within two days of the murders.

They claim some serial killer did it except that serial killer was in jail at the time of the murders.

They claim the police officers lied, the prosecutors lied, the doctors lied, the friend lied on the stand, the social worker lied. In fact, Darlie was lying all along.

Darlie claimed she knew who the intruder was then got up on the stand and admitted she didn't.

They claimed they needed help with expenses even though they had life insurance policies on the murdered children.

They claimed they had to sell everything to pay for Darlie's legal expenses when in truth they really had nothing to sell.

They claimed they lost their house and their business because of the tragedy when in truth they were already behind on both the house payments and the rent payments for the shop.

They claimed that Darlie was a great mom when in truth she would yell at her children to get the hell out of the house.

They claimed the judge was being unfair to Darlie when he moved the trial to a different city. In truth it was Darlie herself, through her lawyer, who requested the change of venue.

Before the murders they claimed to be successful. They were broke.

Before the murders they claimed Darlie was a good mother. In truth she showed her true colors the day two years before the murders when she lost her temper and smashed a piece of birthday cake into her son's face. When he cried and felt embarrassed she snarled at him that he deserved it.

They claimed that they had video from a memorial service that showed Darlie showing appropriate grief shortly after her children were murdered. Yet they never produced the video beyond a thirty second clip that shows Darlie walking around then sitting on the ground while everyone else at the memorial service bowed their heads in prayer.

The prosecutor in Darlie's case is spot on. The jury got it right.

~

If you have any doubt whether Darlie Routier is guilty of capital murder pay close attention to Darlie's own words in the 911 call she made while two of her children lay bleeding to death on the floor right before her eyes.

911 TRANSCRIPT - Recorded by The Rowlett Police Department - June 6, 1996 - Transcript created by Barry Dickey

00:00:00 911 Operator #1 ...Rowlett 911...what is your emergency..

00:01:19 Darlie Routier ...somebody came here...they broke in...

00:03:27 911 Operator #1 ...ma'am...

00:05:11 Darlie Routier ...they just stabbed me and my children...

If your children are bleeding badly and need immediate medical help this is not how you would speak to a 911 Operator. Instead as soon as the operator answered the phone you would scream HELP then say that your children need an ambulance right away and that they have been stabbed. You would then make sure the 911 operator knew your exact address and you would ask what you should do. All of this would take fifteen to thirty seconds, tops.

Not Darlie.

"Somebody came in here..."

"They broke in..."

And then finally Darlie said "They just stabbed me and my children".

This is not normal. Clearly she was getting her story on the recorded line. They broke in. They stabbed me and my children. An honest mother whose children were bleeding to death right before her eyes would have focused only on her children.

HELP! MY CHILDREN HAVE BEEN STABBED. HELP! MY CHILDREN NEED AN AMBULANCE NOW! HELP! MY CHILDREN ARE BLEEDING BADLY AND NEED AN AMBULANCE NOW!

Somebody came in here, they broke in?

00:07:16 911 Operator #1 ...what...

00:08:05 Darlie Routier ...they just stabbed me and my kids...my little boys...

Notice that both times Darlie tells the 911 operator that she and her children have been stabbed she started off with herself. ME and my kids. This isn't normal. A normal mother would have said HELP! MY CHILDREN NEED AN AMBULANCE NOW! THEY'VE BEEN STABBED! THEY ARE BLEEDING BADLY! HERE IS OUR ADDRESS! GET HERE NOW! WHAT CAN I DO TO HELP THEM?

00:09:24 911 Operator #1 ...who...who did...

00:11:12 Darlie Routier ...my little boy is dying...

The 911 operator is obviously shocked by what Darlie is saying. And rightly so. Because if Darlie was truly a mother who had just woken up to a brutal attack by a stranger and her children lay dying right before her eyes this is not how she would have been talking.

Just eleven seconds after dialing 911 Darlie says that her little boy is dying. This is not normal. Parents do not so easily accept the death of their child. Unless of course they are the person who killed them. Instead Darlie would have said that her sons were bleeding badly. And she would have asked for help.

It's interesting to note that Darlie had two sons who were bleeding badly yet her comment was "my little boy is dying".

What follows is the 911 operator dispatching units to the Routier home as fast as possible. Notice Darlie hasn't bothered to make sure the 911 operator knows her address. Notice that Darlie isn't screaming hysterically or demanding the 911 operator's attention in order to get help for her children.

00:11:25 RADIO ...(unintelligible) clear...

00:13:07 911 Operator #1 ...hang on ...hang on... hang on

00:15:03 Darlie Routier ...hurry... (unintelligible)...

00:16:01 911 Operator #1 ...stand by for medical emergency

00:18:11 Darlie Routier ...ma'am...

00:18:19 911 Operator #1 ...hang on ma'am...

00:21:26 Darlie Routier ...ma'am...

00:23:00 911 Operator #1 ...unknown medical emergency... 5801 Eagle Drive...

00:24:00 RADIO ...(unintelligible)...

00:26:24 Darlie Routier ...ma'am...

00:27:12 911 Operator #1 ...ma'am... I'm trying to get an ambulance to you... hang on a minute...

00:28:20 RADIO ...(siren)...

00:29:13 Darlie Routier ...oh my God ...my babies are dying...

Notice how many times Darlie politely says ma'am. This is not a normal reaction from a parent who suddenly discovered that two of her children were so brutally attacked.

00:30:12 Darin Routier ...(unintelligible)...

00:31:09 911 Operator #1 ...what's going on ma'am...

00:32:13 Darlie Routier ...(unintelligible) ...oh my God...

At this point the 911 Operator was able to give Darlie her full attention. She asked what is going on. And Darlie doesn't answer.

00:33:49 RADIO ...(tone - signal broadcast)...

00:34:01 Background Voice ...(unintelligible)...

00:35:20 Darlie Routier ...(unintelligible) thought he was dead ...oh my God...

Pay close attention to Darlie's comment. She said she thought he was dead then said "Oh my God". It seems that perhaps Darlie waited to dial 911 until she believed both of her sons were already dead.

00:39:08 Darin Routier ...(unintelligible)...

00:39:29 Darlie Routier ...I don't even know (unintelligible)...

00:40:22 911 Operator #1 ...attention 901 unknown medical emergency 5801...

00:42:23 Darin Routier ...(unintelligible)...

00:43:15 Darlie Routier ...I don't even know (unintelligible)...

00:44:04 911 Operator #1 ...Eagle Drive ...Box 238 ...cross street Linda Vista and Willowbrook ...attention 901 medial emergency...

00:49:28 Darlie Routier ...who was breathing...

00:40:10 Darin Routier ...(unintelligible)...

00:51:15 Darlie Routier ...(unintelligible) are they still laying there (unintelligible)...

00:51:19 911 Operator #1 ...may be possible stabbing ...5801 Eagle Drive ...Box 238 ...cross street Linda Vista and Willowbrook...

00:55:06 Darlie Routier ...oh my God ...what do we do...

00:57:17 911 Operator #1 ...time out 2:32...

00:58:26 Darlie Routier ...oh my God...

00:58:28 911 Operator #1 ...stamp me a card Clint...

01:01:02 911 Operator #1 ...80...

01:01:16 RADIO ...(unintelligible)...

01:02:13 Darlie Routier ...oh my God...

01:03:05 RADIO ...(unintelligible)...

01:04:07 911 Operator #1 ...need units going towards 5801 Eagle Drive ...5801 Eagle Drive

01:04:07 Darlie Routier ...oh my God ...my baby's dead...

Notice again that Darlie is saying her child is dead. This is not a normal reaction for any parent unless that parent is the person who killed her child. Then just three seconds later she shifts gears and says "hold on honey". So she flips from announcing one of her children is dead to saying hold on to her other child. In my opinion at this point she is trying desperately to sound as if she is a frantic mother on the recorded line.

01:07:08 Darlie Routier ...Damon ...hold on honey...

01:08:11 Darin Routier ...(unintelligible)...

01:08:22 911 Operator #1 ...hysterical female on the phone...

01:10:03 Darlie Routier ...(unintelligible)...

01:10:10 Darin Routier ...(unintelligible)...

01:10:26 911 Operator #1 ...says her child has been stabbed

01:11:28 Darlie Routier ...I saw them Darin...

One of the interesting discrepancies in Darlie's stories is whether there was one intruder or two or perhaps three or four. She says "they" broke in. And now she tells her husband that she saw "them". Yet later she would insist there was just one intruder.

01:12:21 Darin Routier ...oh my God ...(unintelligible) ...came in here...

01:14:10 911 Operator #1 ...ma'am ...I need you to calm down and talk to me...

01:14:24 RADIO ...(unintelligible)...

01:16:25 Darlie Routier ...ok...

01:16:26 SOUND ...(unintelligible)...

01:17:12 911 Operator #1 ...twice Clint...

01:18:26 Darlie Routier ...didn't you get my address...

01:20:19 911 Operator #1 ...5801 Eagle...

01:22:00 Darlie Routier ...yes ...we need help...

Finally, after hanging on the phone and talking about a break in then saying her children were dead Darlie has finally concerned herself with whether or not the 911 Operator knows where the ambulance is needed. And finally Darlie asks for help. But it's interesting that Darlie doesn't say that her children need help. Instead she says "we" need help. It would have been normal for her to have said

MY CHILDREN NEED HELP! MY CHILDREN NEED AN AMBULANCE! MY CHILDREN ARE BLEEDING!"

01:22:03 RADIO ...(unintelligible) will be enroute code...

01:24:20 Darlie Routier ...Darin ...I don't know who it was...

This is interesting considering that while Darlie was in jail waiting for her trial she said that she saw the intruder and she knew who it was.

01:24:23 911 Operator #1 ...2:33 code...

01:26:15 Darlie Routier ...we got to find out who it was...

01:27:12 911 Operator #1 ...ma'am...

01:28:04 911 Operator #1 ...ma'am listen ...listen to me...

01:29:27 Darlie Routier ...yes ...yes ...(unintelligible)...

01:30:23 RADIO ...(unintelligible) I'm clear ...do you need anything...

01:32:08 Darin Routier ...(unintelligible)...

01:32:20 Darlie Routier ...oh my God...

01:34:00 911 Operator #1 ...(unintelligible)...

01:34:22 911 Operator #1 ...do you take the radio Clint...

01:35:23 911 Operator #2 ...yes...

01:36:12 Darlie Routier ...oh my God...

01:36:25 911 Operator #1 ...I...ma'am...

01:38:03 Darlie Routier ...yes...

01:38:17 911 Operator #1 ...I need you to ...

01:38:23 RADIO ...(unintelligible) start that way (unintelligible)... will revise...

01:39:28 911 Operator #1 ...I need you to talk to me...

01:41:21 Darlie Routier ...what ...what ...what...

Darlie is again given the opportunity to have the 911 Operator's full attention and instead of saying HELP, MY CHILDREN ARE BLEEDING, MY CHILDREN NEED AN

AMBULANCE, MY CHILDREN HAVE BEEN STABBED she says "oh my God" and "What... what... what".

01:44:25 RADIO ...(unintelligible)...

01:44:28 Darlie Routier ...my babies are dead (unintelligible)...

This is simply not normal for any parent to so willingly admit that her child is dead. Yet Darlie has repeated that her children are dead over and over again to the 911 operator instead of pleading for an ambulance to be sent immediately to save her children. Also, if she truly believed at that point that her children were dead or were dying as she keeps announcing to the 911 operator and she was not the person who killed them then she would not be hanging on the phone. She would be holding her children.

01:46:20 RADIO ...go ahead and start that way ...siren code 4 ...advise...

01:47:10 Darlie Routier ...(unintelligible)...

01:48:03 Darlie Routier ...(unintelligible) do you want honey ...hold on (unintelligible)...

Now it appears that Darlie is trying to sound like she's talking to one of her children who she has already announced is dead.

01:49:17 911 Operator #1 ...ma'am ...I can't understand you...

01:50:21 Darlie Routier ...yes...

01:51:18 911 Operator #1 ...you're going to have to slow down ...calm down ...and talk to me...

01:52:19 Darlie Routier ...I'm talking to my babies ...they're dying...

She is talking to her dying babies? Really? From across the room? She isn't holding her babies? She isn't applying pressure to their badly bleeding wounds? She isn't cradling them in her arms?

01:55:03 911 Operator #1 ...what is going on...

01:56:29 Darlie Routier ...somebody came in while I was sleeping ...me and my little boys were sleeping downstairs...

Darlie is once again given the 911 operator's full attention and look at what she said. While she was sleeping? She and her little boys were sleeping downstairs?

At this point two minutes have passed already since she first dialed 911. She should have long ago pleaded with the 911 operator to get an ambulance to her house as soon as possible. She should have made sure the 911 operator had her address. And she should have asked the 911 operator what she should do to help her children who were bleeding badly from what appeared to be stab wounds. Darlie did none of what a normal parent would have done. Instead she kept announcing that her children were dead. And then when she had the opportunity to say MY CHILDREN HAVE BEEN STABBED, GET AN AMBULANCE HERE, WHAT SHOULD I DO... Darlie starts her monologue about how she and her children were sleeping downstairs and someone broke into the house. Again I think Darlie is well aware that the phone line is recorded and she is using that phone line to try to get her story officially on record.

02:02:00 RADIO ...(unintelligible) I'll be clear...

02:02:20 Darlie Routier ...some man ...came in ...stabbed my babies ...stabbed me ...I woke up ...I was fighting ...he ran out through the garage ...threw the knife down ...my babies are dying ...they're dead ...oh my God...

02:14:23 911 Operator #1 ...ok ...stay on the phone with me...

02:16:11 Darin Routier ...(unintelligible)...

02:17:06 Darlie Routier ...oh my God...

02:17:29 911 Operator #1 ...what happened (unintelligible) dispatch 901...

02:20:15 Darlie Routier ...hold on honey ...hold on...

02:22:01 911 Operator #1 ...(unintelligible) who was on (unintelligible)...

02:22:26 911 Operator #2 ...it was (unintelligible) the white phone...

02:23:08 Darlie Routier ...hold on...

02:25:26 911 Operator #2 ...they were wondering when we need to dispatch ...so I sent a double team...

02:25:28 Darlie Routier ...oh my God ...oh my God...

02:28:08 911 Operator #1 ...ok ...thanks...

02:28:21 Darlie Routier ...oh my God...

02:29:20 SOUND ...(unintelligible)...

02:30:01 Darlie Routier ...oh my God...

02:30:20 911 Operator #1 ...ma'am...

02:31:06 RADIO ...(unintelligible)...

02:31:14 911 Operator #1 ...who's there with you...

02:32:15 Darlie Routier ...Karen ...(unintelligible)...

02:33:15 911 Operator #1 ...ma'am...

02:34:06 Darlie Routier ...what...

02:38:11 911 Operator #1 ...is there anybody in the house ...besides you and your children...

02:38:11 Darlie Routier ...no ...my husband he just ran downstairs ...he's helping me ...but they're dying ...oh my God ...they're dead...

02:43:24 911 Operator #1 ...ok ...ok ...how many little boys ...is it two boys...

02:46:06 Darin Routier ...(unintelligible)...

02:46:25 Darlie Routier ...there's two of 'em ...there's two...

02:48:18 RADIO ...what's the cross street on that address on Eagle...

Clearly the radio traffic shows they need the cross street. Instead of responding with the name of the cross street or with clear directions to her home Darlie ignores it and throws in another "oh my God".

02:50:15 Darlie Routier ...oh my God ...who would do this...

02:53:13 911 Operator #1 ...(unintelligible) listen to me ...calm down ...(unintelligible)...

02:53:21 Darlie Routier ...I feel really bad ...I think I'm dying...

02:55:06 RADIO ...228...

02:56:06 911 Operator #1 ...go ahead...

02:58:12 RADIO ...(unintelligible) address again (unintelligible)...

02:59:12 RADIO ...(unintelligible)...

02:59:22 Darlie Routier ...when are they going to be here...

It took three full minutes before Darlie acted as if she wanted them to hurry up and get there. Three full minutes. Think about that. Her children are bleeding to death and she is hanging on the phone saying "oh my God" and "my babies are dead" over and over again. Then finally three minutes later she asked how long it would take for help to arrive.

03:00:22 911 Operator #1 ...5801 Eagle Drive ...5801 Eagle Drive...

03:03:28 Darlie Routier ...when are they going to be here...

03:03:29 911 Operator #1 ...going to be a stabbing...

03:05:20 Darlie Routier ...when are they going to be here...

03:06:20 911 Operator #1 ...ma'am ...they're on their way...

03:08:00 RADIO ...(unintelligible)...

03:08:08 Darlie Routier ...I gotta just sit here forever ...oh my God...

??? "I gotta just sit here forever". Her children are dying. And this is what comes out of her mouth?

03:11:14 911 Operator #1 ...2:35...

03:12:05 Darie Routier ...who would do this ...who would do this...

03:13:09 Darin Routier ...(unintelligible)...

03:14:26 911 Operator #1 ...(sounds of typing on computer keyboard)...

03:16:08 911 Operator #1 ...ma'am ...how old are your boys...

03:18:20 Darin Routier ...what...

03:19:03 911 Operator #1 ...how old are your boys...

03:20:04 RADIO ...(unintelligible)...

03:20:21 911 Operator #1 ...no...

03:21:01 Darlie Routier ...seven and five...

03:22:17 911 Operator #1 ...ok...

03:23:08 Darlie Routier ...oh my God ...oh my God ...oh ...he's dead...

03:29:02 911 Operator #1 ...calm down ...can you...

03:29:03 Darlie Routier ...oh God ...Devon no ...oh my God...

03:30:27 SOUND ...(dog barking)...

The dog started barking when the officers entered the house. Obviously had there been an intruder the dog would have started barking as soon as the intruder entered the house.

03:35:02 911 Operator #1 ...is your name Darlie...

03:36:11 Darlie Routier ...yes...

03:36:26 911 Operator #1 ...this is her...

03:37:09 911 Operator #1 ...is your husband's name Darin...

03:38:22 Darlie Routier ...yes ...please hurry ...God they're taking forever...

03:41:20 911 Operator #1 ...there's nobody in your house ...there was ...was...

03:44:05 911 Operator #1 ...you don't know who did this...

03:45:19 Police Officer ...look for a rag...

03:46:11 Darlie Routier ...they killed our babies...

03:48:03 Police Officer ...lay down ...ok ...just sit down ...(unintelligible)

03:51:11 911 Operator #1 ...(sounds of typing on computer keyboard)...

03:52:13 Darlie Routier ...no ...he ran out ...uh ...they ran out in the garage ...I was sleeping...

This is Darlie hanging on the phone ignoring the officer who told her to hang it up and to help her children. She is directing the officer to go check the garage for the intruder and also getting her story straight for the officer that she was sleeping. Her children are laying there dying on the floor and Darlie is pointing toward the garage for the officer to go check it out.

03:54:09 911 Operator #1 ...(unintelligible)...

03:56:19 Darlie Routier ...my babies over here already cut ...can I (unintelligible)...

03:59:29 Darin Routier ...(unintelligible) phone is right there...

04:01:28 Darlie Routier ...(unintelligible)...

04:03:01 RADIO ...(unintelligible)...

04:05:02 Darlie Routier ...ya'll look out in the garage ...look out in the garage ...they left a knife laying on...

04:08:21 RADIO ...(unintelligible)...

04:09:19 911 Operator #1 ...there's a knife ...don't touch anything...

04:11:18 Darlie Routier ...I already touched it and picked it up...

Darlie was very quick to add that she touched the knife. Of course that is important to her case if the investigators are able to get her fingerprints off the knife.

04:12:05 RADIO ...10-4...

04:15:20 911 Operator #1 ...who's out there ...is anybody out there...

04:16:07 Police Officer ...(unintelligible)...

04:17:06 Darlie Routier ...I don't know ...I was sleeping...

04:18:14 911 Operator #1 ...ok ma'am ...listen ...there's a police officer at your front door ...is your front door unlocked...

04:22:11 RADIO ...(unintelligible)...

04:22:15 Darlie Routier ...yes ma'am ...but where's the ambulance...

Darlie was already speaking with the police officers inside her home. Yet she didn't mention that to the 911 operator. Instead she stayed on the line in order to get her story recorded and to try to act like a distraught parent. This entire time her children lay on the floor dying and she didn't go anywhere near them. She would later claim that she laid wet towels on their wounds but according to the first responding officer Darlie didn't go near her children.

04:24:21 911 Operator #1 ...ok...

04:24:23 Darlie Routier ...they're barely breathing...

04:26:17 Darlie Routier ...if they don't get it here they're gonna be dead ...my God they're (unintelligible) ...hurry ...please hurry...

This is simply not how any normal parent would speak. It would be normal to say please hurry or to say hurry as fast as you can because my children are bleeding badly. Tell me what I can do to help them. Or we need an ambulance now. To say "if they don't get it here they're gonna be dead" is simply not at all normal. Parents are not able to so readily accept the death of their child.

04:31:13 911 Operator #1 ...ok ...they're ...they're...

04:32:18 Police Officer ...what about you...

04:33:06 911 Operator #1 ...is 82 out on Eagle...

04:34:18 Darlie Routier ...huh...

04:35:12 Darin Routier ...they took (unintelligible) ...they ran (unintelligible)...

04:36:28 911 Operator #2 ...(unintelligible)...

04:37:08 Darlie Routier ...we're at Eagle ...5801 Eagle ...my God and hurry...

Four minutes and thirty-seven seconds after dialing 911 Darlie FINALLY gives the 911 operator her address.

04:41:03 RADIO ...(unintelligible)...

04:41:22 911 Operator #1 ...82 ...are you out...

04:42:25 Police Officer ...nothing's gone Mrs. Routier...

04:44:10 Darlie Routier ...oh my God ...oh my God ...why would they do this...

04:48:03 RADIO ...(unintelligible) to advise (unintelligible) 200...

04:50:18 Police Officer ...(unintelligible) the problem Mrs. Routier...

04:50:21 911 Operator #1 ...what'd he say...

04:51:29 Darlie Routier ...why would they do this...

04:53:08 Darlie Routier ...I'm (unintelligible)...

04:54:07 911 Operator #1 ...ok ...listen ma'am ...need to ...need to let the officers in the front door ...ok...

04:59:11 Darlie Routier ...what...

05:00:04 911 Operator #1 ...ma'am..

05:00:22 Darlie Routier ...what ...what...

05:01:15 911 Operator #1 ...need to let the police officers in the front door...

05:04:21 Darlie Routier ...(unintelligible) his knife was lying over there and I already picked it up...

The 911 operator told Darlie two more times that she needed to let the officers in. All of this time the officers have already been inside the house and Darlie knows it but she hasn't told the 911 operator. Why? It appears she wants to be able to get her story on the taped line. It also appears that she doesn't want to go anywhere near her children.

05:08:19 911 Operator #1 ...ok ...it's alright ...it's ok...

05:09:20 Darlie Routier ...God ...I bet if we could have gotten the prints maybe ...maybe...

Her children are bleeding to death right before her eyes and she wants to have a discussion about fingerprints on the knife. Notice by her comment that she already believes that her story is convincing that her fingerprints would have interfered with the fake intruder's fingerprints. What she didn't know at the time was that her knife set had handles which made of some sort of material which made it impossible for the police investigators to get any prints off of them. But again, if a parent has two children bleeding to death right before her eyes unless she is the one who stabbed them she would not have been discussing fingerprints on the knife at that very moment. Or at all.

05:13:18 Police Officer ...(unintelligible)...

05:14:18 RADIO ...82 ...we'll be (unintelligible)...

05:17:12 Darlie Routier ...ok ...it'll be...

05:18:08 911 Operator #1 ...ma'am ...hang on ...hang on a second...

05:19:09 Darlie Routier ...somebody who did it intentionally walked in here and did it Darin...

This is perhaps the most revealing segment of the entire 911 call. Darlie's voice changed drastically from a whiny sounding almost helpless sounding person to a person who was angry and very cold. Her husband had just asked her a question and based on her answer and on her angry tone it seems as if he is somehow accusing her of killing their children.

05:20:19 911 Operator #1 ...82 ...10-9...

05:21:23 RADIO ...(unintelligible)...

05:22:28 911 Operator #1 ...received...

05:23:05 Darlie Routier ...there's nothing touched...

05:24:12 911 Operator #1 ...ok ma'am...

05:25:13 Darlie Routier ...there's nothing touched...

05:26:20 RADIO ...(unintelligible)...

05:28:00 Darlie Routier ...oh my God...

05:29:08 Police Officer ...(unintelligible)...

05:29:23 RADIO ...received...

05:31:19 RADIO ...(unintelligible)...

05:33:25 911 Operator #1 ...ma'am ...is the police officer there...

05:35:14 Darlie Routier ...yes (unintelligible)...

05:35:23 911 Operator #1 ...ok ...go talk to him ...ok...

05:38:03 RADIO ...(unintelligible)...

Finally Darlie admitted the police officer was there. The actual call was over six minutes long and the police officer had arrived shortly after three minutes into the call. Yet darlie stayed on the phone and when the 911 operator repeatedly told her to open the door for the officer Darlie repeatedly acted as if she didn't know the police officer was already there.

At the tail end of the 911 call Darlie had to be told twice by the 911 operator to get off the phone and to go talk to the police officer. Finally Darlie didn't have an excuse to avoid helping her children.

Remember that finally at the three and a half minute mark the family dog started to bark. That's because the police officers were entering the house at that point. And remember the family dog was a known barker. In fact he even tried to bite one of the police officers.

But if you want to believe Darlie's story then you would have to believe that the same dog would have just sat there while an intruder broke into the house, brutally stabbed two little boys, slashed Darlie's throat then walked through the house toward the garage.

Baloney.

Also notice on the 911 call how Darlie was very quick to say that her children were dying. This is not normal behavior for a parent. Now take a second look at the 911 call from the perspective that Darlie is guilty of murdering her children. And suddenly her statements to the 911 operator make sense. She doesn't hold her children. When the officers arrive she doesn't get off the phone. When the officer tells her to get off the phone and to help her children she flat out ignores him and continues to hang on the line.

She doesn't say that her children have been stabbed and need an ambulance immediately. She said that "They broke in" and stabbed her and her children. She doesn't make sure the 911 operator knows her address. She doesn't ask what she can do to help her children. She doesn't apply pressure to her children's wounds.

She doesn't try to save her children.

And when it is obvious to her that her children are dying she doesn't get off the phone in order to comfort her children.

When it is obvious to her that her children are dying she starts talking about the knife that might have her fingerprints on it.

Darlie Routier thought she could get away with murder. But the Rowlett Police Department was on to her from the start. According to Darlie's followers the investigators unfairly targeted Darlie. But that is simply not true. They fully investigated the case. They followed every lead. They also surmised early on in the investigation that the crime scene did not appear to show evidence of any intruder. So they ran a parallel investigation to check out both Darlie and her husband too. They interviewed many people who knew Darlie and her family. They investigated Darlie's husband thoroughly then cleared him from any suspicion of being involved in the murders of his children. Then they set their sights more closely on Darlie and when all of the evidence, both physical and circumstantial, pointed to Darlie as being the person who murdered her children, the police arrested Darlie and charged her with murder.

The investigators did their jobs. And they did their jobs well. The prosecutors did their jobs and they also did their jobs well. And the jurors who voted unanimously that Darlie was guilty of capital murder got it right.

Remember that even though Darlie's followers will say that she had no idea she was a suspect so she went ahead and spoke with the police without a lawyer by her side that it simply is not true. The truth is that within one hour of leaving the hospital Darlie was taken to the police station and given the Miranda warning.

Darlie's followers will say that Darlie was a great mom who doted on her children. Also not true considering that her children were begging to not have to be near her the day before they were murdered.

Darlie's followers will say that she fixed her children a nice big dinner the evening before they were murdered. In fact the children were fed a bowl of soup and they were seated at a separate table from Darlie.

Darlie's followers will say that there was a suspicious black car in the neighborhood that the police investigators never investigated. In fact there was a couple driving through the area who were interested in landscaping their own yard and wanted to get some good landscaping ideas.

Darlie's followers will say that a serial killer who was known to break in and kill children is responsible for the crime. In fact the person they are talking about was in prison at the time.

Darlie's followers claim that in the morning hours of Darlie's big cemetery party that she was videotaped crying at a memorial service for her boys. Yet in the last twenty years they have failed to produce any clip of the supposed video which would show that Darlie had ever shown any grief over losing her children. In fact the clip they have released shows Darlie walking around then plopping down on the ground while the other attendees all had their heads bowed in prayer.

Darlie's followers claim that the judge in her case took sixteen naps during her trial. Yet, the only person to claim she saw the judge actually napping was one of Darlie's husband's aunts. Nobody else in the courtroom noticed the judge taking any naps.

Darlie's followers claim that the trial transcripts cannot be trusted yet the court verified the transcripts for accuracy.

Darlie's followers say the knife used to cut the screen did not come from Darlie's kitchen even though the investigators found particles on a knife taken from Darlie's kitchen consistent with the screen material.

Darlie's followers claim there was an intruder who murdered Darlie's children yet the physical evidence at the crime scene proves the murderer was Darlie herself.

Sometimes Darlie's followers claim that she fought off her intruder. Other times they claim she was drugged throughout the ordeal. And still other times they claim she suffers from traumatic memory lapses so of course she can't remember whether she fought off the intruder or not.

The prosecutor in Darlie's case nailed it when he said that every five years her family comes up with another story yet they fail to ever produce any proof to substantiate their claims. And as I stated earlier their latest claim is that Darlie's husband is the person who murdered his children. If he knows what Darlie did to their children as one of their closest friends insists he does then he should come forward and tell the police officers and the prosecutors what he knows.

If Darlie's husband attempted to cover up for her after she murdered their children then he should do the right thing and tell the truth. The police officers deserve for him to tell the truth. The prosecutors deserve for him to tell the truth. The jurors deserve for him to tell the truth.

But most importantly his only surviving son deserves to know the truth that on that day so long ago while he was safely tucked in his crib in his parents' bedroom that it was none other than his own mother who so brutally took his older brothers' lives.

He deserves to know the truth about what happened to his brothers. And he deserves to hear the truth from his own dad.

Made in the USA
Monee, IL
14 September 2023